Comfort in a Bowl: 50 Hearty Stew Recipes

By: Kelly Johnson

Table of Contents

- Classic Beef Stew
- Chicken and Dumplings Stew
- Lamb and Barley Stew
- Irish Stew with Guinness
- Pork and Sweet Potato Stew
- Seafood Cioppino
- Hungarian Goulash
- Moroccan Lamb Tagine
- Vegetable Lentil Stew
- Brunswick Stew
- Tuscan White Bean Stew
- Chicken Cacciatore Stew
- Sausage and Kale Stew
- Creole Shrimp Stew
- Mushroom and Barley Stew
- Pumpkin and Chickpea Stew
- Venison Stew with Root Vegetables
- Thai Green Curry Stew
- Slow-Cooked Oxtail Stew
- Sweet Potato and Black Bean Stew
- Spicy Chorizo and Potato Stew
- Beef Bourguignon
- Ham and Navy Bean Stew
- Coconut Chicken Stew
- Zucchini and Tomato Stew
- Korean Spicy Beef Stew (Yukgaejang)
- Cajun Crawfish Stew
- Italian Sausage and White Bean Stew
- Salmon and Leek Stew
- Eggplant and Chickpea Stew
- Spicy Peanut and Chicken Stew
- Green Chile Pork Stew
- Caribbean Goat Stew
- Ratatouille Stew
- Braised Short Rib Stew

- Lentil and Spinach Stew
- Curried Beef and Potato Stew
- Hearty Turkey Stew
- Southwestern Chicken and Corn Stew
- Indian Butter Chicken Stew
- French Provençal Stew (Daube)
- Smoky Black Bean Stew
- Crab and Corn Stew
- Hearty Meatball Stew
- Italian Polenta and Sausage Stew
- Spicy Tomato and Egg Stew
- Jamaican Red Pea Stew
- Persian Lamb and Apricot Stew
- Roasted Cauliflower and Coconut Stew
- Wild Mushroom and Herb Stew

Classic Beef Stew

Ingredients:

- 2 lbs beef chuck, cubed
- 4 medium carrots, sliced
- 3 medium potatoes, cubed
- 1 medium onion, diced
- 3 cloves garlic, minced
- 4 cups beef broth
- 2 tablespoons tomato paste
- 2 tablespoons olive oil
- 1 tablespoon Worcestershire sauce
- 1 teaspoon dried thyme
- 2 bay leaves
- Salt and pepper to taste

Instructions:

Heat olive oil in a large pot over medium heat. Brown the beef cubes, then remove and set aside. Sauté onion and garlic until softened. Stir in tomato paste, thyme, and bay leaves, cooking for 1 minute. Return beef to the pot, add beef broth and Worcestershire sauce, and bring to a simmer. Add carrots and potatoes, cover, and simmer for 1.5-2 hours, or until the beef is tender. Season with salt and pepper and serve warm.

Chicken and Dumplings Stew

Ingredients:

- 1 lb chicken thighs, diced
- 2 medium carrots, sliced
- 2 stalks celery, sliced
- 1 medium onion, diced
- 4 cups chicken broth
- 1 cup milk
- 1/3 cup all-purpose flour
- 1 teaspoon dried parsley
- Salt and pepper to taste

Dumplings:

- 1 cup all-purpose flour
- 2 teaspoons baking powder
- 1/4 teaspoon salt
- 1/2 cup milk
- 2 tablespoons melted butter

Instructions:

In a pot, cook chicken until browned, then set aside. Sauté onion, carrots, and celery until softened. Stir in flour and cook for 1 minute. Add chicken broth, milk, and parsley, and bring to a simmer. Add chicken back into the pot. For dumplings, mix dry ingredients, then stir in milk and butter. Drop spoonfuls of dumpling batter onto the simmering stew, cover, and cook for 15 minutes. Season with salt and pepper before serving.

Lamb and Barley Stew

Ingredients:

- 1.5 lbs lamb shoulder, cubed
- 1 cup pearl barley
- 2 medium carrots, diced
- 2 medium potatoes, diced
- 1 medium onion, diced
- 4 cups lamb or beef broth
- 1 teaspoon dried rosemary
- 2 tablespoons olive oil
- Salt and pepper to taste

Instructions:

Brown the lamb in olive oil, then set aside. Sauté onion, carrots, and potatoes in the same pot until softened. Add the lamb back in, along with barley, rosemary, and broth. Bring to a boil, then reduce heat and simmer for 1.5-2 hours, or until the lamb and barley are tender. Season with salt and pepper and serve hot.

Irish Stew with Guinness

Ingredients:

- 2 lbs lamb or beef, cubed
- 4 medium potatoes, cubed
- 2 medium carrots, sliced
- 1 medium onion, diced
- 2 cloves garlic, minced
- 2 cups Guinness beer
- 2 cups beef broth
- 2 tablespoons tomato paste
- 1 tablespoon olive oil
- 1 teaspoon dried thyme
- Salt and pepper to taste

Instructions:

Heat olive oil in a pot and brown the meat. Remove and set aside. Sauté onion and garlic, then stir in tomato paste and thyme. Add Guinness, beef broth, meat, potatoes, and carrots. Bring to a boil, then reduce heat and simmer for 2 hours, or until the meat is tender. Season with salt and pepper before serving.

Pork and Sweet Potato Stew

Ingredients:

- 1 lb pork shoulder, cubed
- 2 medium sweet potatoes, cubed
- 1 medium onion, diced
- 3 cloves garlic, minced
- 4 cups chicken broth
- 1 teaspoon smoked paprika
- 2 tablespoons olive oil
- Salt and pepper to taste

Instructions:

Brown the pork in olive oil and set aside. Sauté onion and garlic until softened. Stir in sweet potatoes, paprika, and chicken broth. Add the pork back to the pot and bring to a simmer. Cook for 1.5 hours, or until the pork is tender. Season with salt and pepper before serving.

Seafood Cioppino

Ingredients:

- 1 lb mixed seafood (shrimp, scallops, mussels, etc.)
- 1 medium onion, diced
- 3 cloves garlic, minced
- 2 cups crushed tomatoes
- 4 cups seafood broth
- 1 cup white wine
- 2 tablespoons olive oil
- 1 teaspoon red pepper flakes
- Salt and pepper to taste

Instructions:

Heat olive oil in a pot and sauté onion and garlic. Stir in crushed tomatoes, seafood broth, wine, and red pepper flakes. Simmer for 15 minutes. Add seafood and cook for 5-7 minutes, or until the seafood is cooked through. Season with salt and pepper and serve with crusty bread.

Hungarian Goulash

Ingredients:

- 2 lbs beef chuck, cubed
- 2 medium potatoes, cubed
- 1 medium onion, diced
- 3 cloves garlic, minced
- 2 tablespoons Hungarian paprika
- 4 cups beef broth
- 2 tablespoons olive oil
- Salt and pepper to taste

Instructions:

Brown the beef in olive oil and set aside. Sauté onion and garlic, then stir in paprika. Add beef broth, meat, and potatoes. Simmer for 1.5-2 hours, or until the beef is tender. Season with salt and pepper before serving.

Moroccan Lamb Tagine

Ingredients:

- 2 lbs lamb, cubed
- 1 medium onion, diced
- 2 medium carrots, sliced
- 1/2 cup dried apricots, chopped
- 2 cups chicken broth
- 1 teaspoon ground cinnamon
- 1 teaspoon ground cumin
- 2 tablespoons olive oil
- Salt and pepper to taste

Instructions:

Brown the lamb in olive oil and set aside. Sauté onion and carrots, then stir in cinnamon and cumin. Add lamb, apricots, and chicken broth. Simmer for 1.5 hours, or until the lamb is tender. Season with salt and pepper and serve with couscous.

Vegetable Lentil Stew

Ingredients:

- 1 cup lentils, rinsed
- 2 medium carrots, diced
- 2 medium potatoes, diced
- 1 medium onion, diced
- 3 cloves garlic, minced
- 4 cups vegetable broth
- 1 teaspoon smoked paprika
- 1 tablespoon olive oil
- Salt and pepper to taste

Instructions:

Heat olive oil in a pot and sauté onion, carrots, and garlic. Stir in potatoes, lentils, paprika, and vegetable broth. Bring to a boil, then reduce heat and simmer for 30 minutes, or until lentils are tender. Season with salt and pepper before serving.

Brunswick Stew

Ingredients:

- 1 lb shredded chicken
- 1 lb pulled pork
- 1 medium onion, diced
- 2 cups frozen lima beans
- 2 cups frozen corn
- 4 cups chicken broth
- 2 cups diced tomatoes
- 1/4 cup barbecue sauce
- 2 tablespoons tomato paste
- 1 tablespoon Worcestershire sauce
- Salt and pepper to taste

Instructions:

Sauté onion in a large pot until softened. Add chicken broth, tomatoes, tomato paste, barbecue sauce, and Worcestershire sauce. Stir in chicken, pork, lima beans, and corn. Simmer for 30–40 minutes, stirring occasionally. Season with salt and pepper before serving.

Tuscan White Bean Stew

Ingredients:

- 2 cups canned cannellini beans, drained
- 1 medium onion, diced
- 3 cloves garlic, minced
- 1 cup diced tomatoes
- 4 cups vegetable broth
- 2 cups kale, chopped
- 1 teaspoon dried thyme
- 2 tablespoons olive oil
- Salt and pepper to taste

Instructions:

Sauté onion and garlic in olive oil until fragrant. Add tomatoes, thyme, and vegetable broth, then stir in beans. Simmer for 10 minutes, then add kale and cook for another 5 minutes. Season with salt and pepper before serving.

Chicken Cacciatore Stew

Ingredients:

- 1 lb chicken thighs, diced
- 1 medium onion, diced
- 3 cloves garlic, minced
- 1 cup diced tomatoes
- 1/2 cup chicken broth
- 1/2 cup red wine
- 1 bell pepper, sliced
- 1 teaspoon dried oregano
- 2 tablespoons olive oil
- Salt and pepper to taste

Instructions:

Brown chicken in olive oil, then remove and set aside. Sauté onion, garlic, and bell pepper in the same pot. Add tomatoes, chicken broth, wine, and oregano. Return chicken to the pot, cover, and simmer for 30 minutes. Season with salt and pepper before serving.

Sausage and Kale Stew

Ingredients:

- 1 lb Italian sausage, sliced
- 2 medium potatoes, diced
- 1 medium onion, diced
- 3 cloves garlic, minced
- 4 cups chicken broth
- 2 cups kale, chopped
- 1 teaspoon smoked paprika
- Salt and pepper to taste

Instructions:

Brown sausage in a pot and set aside. Sauté onion and garlic in the same pot until softened. Add chicken broth, potatoes, and paprika. Simmer for 15 minutes, then stir in sausage and kale. Cook for another 5 minutes, season, and serve.

Creole Shrimp Stew

Ingredients:

- 1 lb shrimp, peeled and deveined
- 1 medium onion, diced
- 1 green bell pepper, diced
- 3 cloves garlic, minced
- 2 cups diced tomatoes
- 4 cups chicken broth
- 1 tablespoon Creole seasoning
- 1 tablespoon olive oil
- Salt and pepper to taste

Instructions:

Sauté onion, bell pepper, and garlic in olive oil until softened. Add tomatoes, chicken broth, and Creole seasoning. Simmer for 10 minutes, then add shrimp. Cook for 5–7 minutes, or until shrimp are opaque. Season and serve with rice.

Mushroom and Barley Stew

Ingredients:

- 1 lb mushrooms, sliced
- 1 cup pearl barley
- 1 medium onion, diced
- 2 cloves garlic, minced
- 4 cups vegetable broth
- 1 teaspoon dried thyme
- 2 tablespoons olive oil
- Salt and pepper to taste

Instructions:

Sauté mushrooms, onion, and garlic in olive oil until softened. Add barley, thyme, and vegetable broth. Simmer for 30–40 minutes, or until barley is tender. Season with salt and pepper before serving.

Pumpkin and Chickpea Stew

Ingredients:

- 2 cups pumpkin, diced
- 1 cup canned chickpeas, drained
- 1 medium onion, diced
- 3 cloves garlic, minced
- 4 cups vegetable broth
- 1 teaspoon ground cumin
- 1 teaspoon smoked paprika
- 2 tablespoons olive oil
- Salt and pepper to taste

Instructions:

Sauté onion and garlic in olive oil. Add pumpkin, chickpeas, cumin, paprika, and vegetable broth. Simmer for 20–25 minutes, or until pumpkin is tender. Season with salt and pepper before serving.

Venison Stew with Root Vegetables

Ingredients:

- 1 lb venison, cubed
- 2 medium potatoes, diced
- 2 medium carrots, sliced
- 1 medium parsnip, diced
- 1 medium onion, diced
- 4 cups beef broth
- 1 teaspoon dried rosemary
- 2 tablespoons olive oil
- Salt and pepper to taste

Instructions:

Brown venison in olive oil and set aside. Sauté onion in the same pot, then add root vegetables, rosemary, and beef broth. Return venison to the pot and simmer for 1.5 hours, or until tender. Season with salt and pepper before serving.

Thai Green Curry Stew

Ingredients:

- 1 lb chicken, diced
- 1 medium onion, diced
- 2 cups coconut milk
- 2 tablespoons green curry paste
- 1 cup green beans, trimmed
- 1 cup zucchini, sliced
- 1 tablespoon fish sauce
- 1 tablespoon olive oil

Instructions:

Sauté chicken and onion in olive oil until cooked. Stir in curry paste, then add coconut milk, green beans, and zucchini. Simmer for 10 minutes. Stir in fish sauce, adjust seasoning, and serve over rice.

Slow-Cooked Oxtail Stew

Ingredients:

- 2 lbs oxtail, cut into pieces
- 1 large onion, chopped
- 3 cloves garlic, minced
- 4 cups beef broth
- 2 medium carrots, sliced
- 2 celery stalks, chopped
- 2 medium potatoes, diced
- 1 teaspoon dried thyme
- 1 bay leaf
- Salt and pepper to taste

Instructions:

Season the oxtail with salt and pepper. In a skillet, brown the oxtail pieces on all sides. Transfer the oxtail to a slow cooker and add all the remaining ingredients. Cook on low for 8–10 hours or until the meat is tender and falling off the bone. Adjust seasoning with salt and pepper before serving.

Sweet Potato and Black Bean Stew

Ingredients:

- 2 medium sweet potatoes, peeled and diced
- 1 can black beans, drained and rinsed
- 1 medium onion, chopped
- 3 cloves garlic, minced
- 4 cups vegetable broth
- 1 teaspoon ground cumin
- 1 teaspoon chili powder
- 2 tablespoons olive oil
- Salt and pepper to taste

Instructions:

Heat olive oil in a large pot, then sauté onion and garlic until softened. Add sweet potatoes, black beans, cumin, chili powder, and vegetable broth. Bring to a boil, then reduce heat and simmer for 25–30 minutes, or until the sweet potatoes are tender. Season with salt and pepper and serve.

Spicy Chorizo and Potato Stew

Ingredients:

- 1 lb chorizo sausage, casing removed
- 4 medium potatoes, diced
- 1 medium onion, chopped
- 3 cloves garlic, minced
- 4 cups chicken broth
- 1 teaspoon smoked paprika
- 1/2 teaspoon cayenne pepper
- 2 tablespoons olive oil
- Salt and pepper to taste

Instructions:

In a large pot, brown the chorizo in olive oil. Remove and set aside. In the same pot, sauté onion and garlic until softened. Add potatoes, smoked paprika, cayenne pepper, and chicken broth. Bring to a boil, then reduce heat and simmer for 20–25 minutes, or until potatoes are tender. Stir in chorizo, adjust seasoning, and serve.

Beef Bourguignon

Ingredients:

- 2 lbs beef stew meat, cubed
- 1 bottle red wine (Burgundy or Pinot Noir)
- 1 large onion, chopped
- 3 cloves garlic, minced
- 2 cups beef broth
- 2 cups carrots, sliced
- 1/2 lb mushrooms, sliced
- 2 tablespoons tomato paste
- 2 tablespoons flour
- 1 bay leaf
- 1 teaspoon dried thyme
- 1 tablespoon olive oil
- Salt and pepper to taste

Instructions:

In a large Dutch oven, brown the beef in olive oil. Remove and set aside. Sauté onion and garlic in the same pot, then add tomato paste and flour. Stir to combine, then add wine, beef broth, carrots, mushrooms, and seasonings. Return beef to the pot and bring to a boil. Cover, reduce heat, and simmer for 2–3 hours, or until the beef is tender. Season with salt and pepper before serving.

Ham and Navy Bean Stew

Ingredients:

- 2 cups cooked ham, diced
- 2 cups navy beans, soaked overnight
- 1 medium onion, chopped
- 3 cloves garlic, minced
- 4 cups chicken broth
- 2 medium carrots, sliced
- 1 celery stalk, chopped
- 1 teaspoon dried thyme
- 1 bay leaf
- Salt and pepper to taste

Instructions:

In a large pot, sauté onion and garlic until softened. Add ham, beans, chicken broth, carrots, celery, thyme, and bay leaf. Bring to a boil, then reduce heat and simmer for 1.5 to 2 hours, or until the beans are tender. Season with salt and pepper before serving.

Coconut Chicken Stew

Ingredients:

- 1 lb chicken thighs, boneless and skinless, cut into chunks
- 1 medium onion, chopped
- 2 cloves garlic, minced
- 1 can coconut milk
- 2 cups chicken broth
- 1 medium sweet potato, peeled and diced
- 1 teaspoon ground ginger
- 1 teaspoon ground turmeric
- 2 tablespoons olive oil
- Salt and pepper to taste

Instructions:

In a large pot, sauté onion and garlic in olive oil until softened. Add chicken, sweet potato, ginger, turmeric, coconut milk, and chicken broth. Bring to a boil, then reduce heat and simmer for 25–30 minutes, or until the chicken is cooked through and the sweet potato is tender. Season with salt and pepper before serving.

Zucchini and Tomato Stew

Ingredients:

- 2 medium zucchinis, diced
- 4 medium tomatoes, chopped
- 1 medium onion, chopped
- 3 cloves garlic, minced
- 4 cups vegetable broth
- 1 teaspoon dried oregano
- 2 tablespoons olive oil
- Salt and pepper to taste

Instructions:

In a large pot, sauté onion and garlic in olive oil until softened. Add zucchini, tomatoes, vegetable broth, and oregano. Bring to a boil, then reduce heat and simmer for 20 minutes. Season with salt and pepper before serving.

Korean Spicy Beef Stew (Yukgaejang)

Ingredients:

- 1 lb beef brisket, thinly sliced
- 1 onion, sliced
- 3 cloves garlic, minced
- 1 tablespoon ginger, minced
- 2 tablespoons gochujang (Korean chili paste)
- 1 tablespoon soy sauce
- 4 cups beef broth
- 1 cup bean sprouts
- 2 cups spinach
- 2 green onions, chopped
- 1 tablespoon sesame oil
- 1 teaspoon sesame seeds
- Salt and pepper to taste

Instructions:

In a large pot, sauté beef brisket, onion, garlic, and ginger in sesame oil until beef is browned. Stir in gochujang, soy sauce, and beef broth. Bring to a boil, then reduce heat and simmer for 1–1.5 hours, or until the beef is tender. Add bean sprouts, spinach, and green onions, then cook for another 5 minutes. Sprinkle with sesame seeds and adjust seasoning with salt and pepper before serving.

Cajun Crawfish Stew

Ingredients:

- 1 lb crawfish tails, peeled
- 1 medium onion, chopped
- 1 bell pepper, chopped
- 3 cloves garlic, minced
- 2 cups chicken broth
- 1 can diced tomatoes (14.5 oz)
- 1 teaspoon Cajun seasoning
- 1 teaspoon paprika
- 1/2 teaspoon thyme
- 2 tablespoons olive oil
- Salt and pepper to taste

Instructions:

In a large pot, heat olive oil and sauté onion, bell pepper, and garlic until softened. Add the diced tomatoes, chicken broth, Cajun seasoning, paprika, thyme, salt, and pepper. Bring to a boil, then reduce heat and simmer for 15–20 minutes. Stir in crawfish tails and cook for an additional 5–10 minutes, or until the crawfish are fully cooked. Adjust seasoning and serve.

Italian Sausage and White Bean Stew

Ingredients:

- 1 lb Italian sausage, casing removed
- 2 cups white beans (canned or cooked from dry)
- 1 medium onion, chopped
- 3 cloves garlic, minced
- 4 cups chicken broth
- 2 cups spinach, chopped
- 1 teaspoon dried oregano
- 1/2 teaspoon red pepper flakes
- 2 tablespoons olive oil
- Salt and pepper to taste

Instructions:

In a large pot, heat olive oil and brown the sausage over medium heat. Remove the sausage and set aside. In the same pot, sauté onion and garlic until softened. Add the beans, chicken broth, oregano, and red pepper flakes. Bring to a boil, then reduce heat and simmer for 15 minutes. Stir in spinach and sausage, and cook for an additional 5 minutes. Adjust seasoning with salt and pepper before serving.

Salmon and Leek Stew

Ingredients:

- 1 lb salmon fillets, skin removed and cut into chunks
- 2 medium leeks, cleaned and sliced
- 2 cups potatoes, diced
- 4 cups fish stock or vegetable broth
- 1 cup heavy cream
- 2 tablespoons olive oil
- 1 tablespoon fresh dill, chopped
- Salt and pepper to taste

Instructions:

In a large pot, heat olive oil and sauté leeks until softened. Add the potatoes and fish stock, then bring to a boil. Reduce heat and simmer for 10–15 minutes, or until the potatoes are tender. Stir in the salmon chunks and cook for another 5–7 minutes, until the salmon is cooked through. Stir in the heavy cream, dill, and season with salt and pepper before serving.

Eggplant and Chickpea Stew

Ingredients:

- 2 medium eggplants, diced
- 1 can chickpeas, drained and rinsed
- 1 medium onion, chopped
- 3 cloves garlic, minced
- 1 can diced tomatoes (14.5 oz)
- 4 cups vegetable broth
- 1 teaspoon ground cumin
- 1 teaspoon ground coriander
- 1 tablespoon olive oil
- Salt and pepper to taste

Instructions:

In a large pot, heat olive oil and sauté onion and garlic until softened. Add the eggplant and cook until lightly browned. Stir in the chickpeas, diced tomatoes, vegetable broth, cumin, and coriander. Bring to a boil, then reduce heat and simmer for 20–25 minutes, or until the eggplant is tender. Season with salt and pepper and serve.

Spicy Peanut and Chicken Stew

Ingredients:

- 1 lb chicken thighs, boneless and skinless, cut into chunks
- 1 medium onion, chopped
- 3 cloves garlic, minced
- 1 can diced tomatoes (14.5 oz)
- 1 cup peanut butter (creamy)
- 4 cups chicken broth
- 1 teaspoon ground ginger
- 1 teaspoon cayenne pepper
- 2 tablespoons olive oil
- Salt and pepper to taste

Instructions:

In a large pot, heat olive oil and brown the chicken pieces on all sides. Remove chicken and set aside. In the same pot, sauté onion and garlic until softened. Add diced tomatoes, peanut butter, chicken broth, ginger, and cayenne pepper. Stir to combine, then bring to a boil. Reduce heat and simmer for 25–30 minutes, until the chicken is cooked through. Season with salt and pepper before serving.

Green Chile Pork Stew

Ingredients:

- 2 lbs pork shoulder, cubed
- 1 medium onion, chopped
- 3 cloves garlic, minced
- 2 cups green chile, chopped (or canned green chiles)
- 4 cups chicken broth
- 1 teaspoon cumin
- 1/2 teaspoon oregano
- 2 tablespoons olive oil
- Salt and pepper to taste

Instructions:

In a large pot, heat olive oil and brown the pork cubes on all sides. Remove and set aside. In the same pot, sauté onion and garlic until softened. Add green chile, chicken broth, cumin, oregano, and pork. Bring to a boil, then reduce heat and simmer for 1.5 to 2 hours, or until the pork is tender. Adjust seasoning with salt and pepper before serving.

Caribbean Goat Stew

Ingredients:

- 2 lbs goat meat, cubed
- 1 medium onion, chopped
- 3 cloves garlic, minced
- 2 medium carrots, chopped
- 2 cups coconut milk
- 2 cups beef broth
- 1 teaspoon thyme
- 1 teaspoon allspice
- 2 tablespoons curry powder
- 2 tablespoons vegetable oil
- Salt and pepper to taste

Instructions:

In a large pot, heat vegetable oil and brown the goat meat on all sides. Remove and set aside. In the same pot, sauté onion, garlic, and carrots until softened. Stir in thyme, allspice, curry powder, coconut milk, beef broth, and the browned goat meat. Bring to a boil, then reduce heat and simmer for 2–3 hours, or until the goat meat is tender. Season with salt and pepper and serve.

Ratatouille Stew

Ingredients:

- 1 medium eggplant, diced
- 2 medium zucchini, diced
- 1 bell pepper, chopped
- 2 medium tomatoes, chopped
- 1 onion, chopped
- 3 cloves garlic, minced
- 4 tablespoons olive oil
- 1 teaspoon dried thyme
- 1/2 teaspoon dried oregano
- Salt and pepper to taste

Instructions:

In a large pot, heat olive oil and sauté onion, garlic, eggplant, zucchini, and bell pepper until softened. Add tomatoes, thyme, oregano, salt, and pepper. Stir to combine, then reduce heat and simmer for 20–25 minutes, or until all vegetables are tender. Adjust seasoning before serving.

Braised Short Rib Stew

Ingredients:

- 2 lbs beef short ribs
- 1 medium onion, chopped
- 3 cloves garlic, minced
- 4 cups beef broth
- 2 cups red wine
- 2 tablespoons tomato paste
- 2 medium carrots, chopped
- 2 tablespoons olive oil
- 1 tablespoon fresh rosemary, chopped
- Salt and pepper to taste

Instructions:

In a large pot, heat olive oil and brown the short ribs on all sides. Remove and set aside. In the same pot, sauté onion and garlic until softened. Stir in tomato paste and cook for 2 minutes. Add beef broth, red wine, carrots, rosemary, salt, and pepper. Return short ribs to the pot and bring to a boil. Reduce heat and simmer for 2–3 hours, or until the meat is tender. Season with additional salt and pepper before serving.

Lentil and Spinach Stew

Ingredients:

- 1 1/2 cups lentils, rinsed
- 4 cups vegetable broth
- 1 medium onion, chopped
- 3 cloves garlic, minced
- 2 cups spinach, chopped
- 2 medium carrots, diced
- 1 teaspoon cumin
- 1 teaspoon turmeric
- 2 tablespoons olive oil
- Salt and pepper to taste

Instructions:

In a large pot, heat olive oil and sauté onion, garlic, and carrots until softened. Stir in cumin and turmeric, and cook for another minute. Add lentils and vegetable broth, and bring to a boil. Reduce heat and simmer for 25-30 minutes, or until lentils are tender. Stir in spinach and cook for an additional 5 minutes. Season with salt and pepper before serving.

Curried Beef and Potato Stew

Ingredients:

- 1 lb beef stew meat, cubed
- 2 medium potatoes, peeled and diced
- 1 medium onion, chopped
- 3 cloves garlic, minced
- 2 tablespoons curry powder
- 4 cups beef broth
- 1 can diced tomatoes (14.5 oz)
- 1 tablespoon fresh cilantro, chopped
- 2 tablespoons olive oil
- Salt and pepper to taste

Instructions:

In a large pot, heat olive oil and brown the beef cubes on all sides. Remove the beef and set aside. In the same pot, sauté onion and garlic until softened. Stir in curry powder and cook for 1 minute. Add potatoes, beef broth, diced tomatoes, and beef back into the pot. Bring to a boil, then reduce heat and simmer for 1 hour, or until the beef is tender and the potatoes are cooked through. Season with salt, pepper, and cilantro before serving.

Hearty Turkey Stew

Ingredients:

- 1 lb turkey breast or thighs, cubed
- 4 cups chicken broth
- 2 medium carrots, diced
- 2 celery stalks, chopped
- 1 medium onion, chopped
- 3 cloves garlic, minced
- 1 teaspoon thyme
- 1/2 teaspoon rosemary
- 2 tablespoons olive oil
- Salt and pepper to taste

Instructions:

In a large pot, heat olive oil and brown the turkey cubes on all sides. Remove and set aside. In the same pot, sauté onion, garlic, carrots, and celery until softened. Stir in thyme, rosemary, and turkey. Add chicken broth and bring to a boil. Reduce heat and simmer for 30–40 minutes, or until the turkey is tender and the vegetables are cooked. Season with salt and pepper before serving.

Southwestern Chicken and Corn Stew

Ingredients:

- 1 lb chicken breast or thighs, diced
- 2 cups corn kernels (fresh or frozen)
- 1 medium onion, chopped
- 1 bell pepper, chopped
- 1 can diced tomatoes (14.5 oz)
- 4 cups chicken broth
- 1 teaspoon cumin
- 1 teaspoon chili powder
- 1/2 teaspoon smoked paprika
- 2 tablespoons olive oil
- Salt and pepper to taste

Instructions:

In a large pot, heat olive oil and sauté onion, bell pepper, and chicken until browned. Add cumin, chili powder, smoked paprika, diced tomatoes, corn, and chicken broth. Bring to a boil, then reduce heat and simmer for 25–30 minutes, or until the chicken is cooked through and the flavors have melded together. Season with salt and pepper before serving.

Indian Butter Chicken Stew

Ingredients:

- 1 lb chicken breast or thighs, cubed
- 1 medium onion, chopped
- 3 cloves garlic, minced
- 1 tablespoon ginger, grated
- 1 can diced tomatoes (14.5 oz)
- 1 cup heavy cream
- 2 tablespoons butter
- 1 tablespoon garam masala
- 1 teaspoon turmeric
- 1 teaspoon ground cumin
- 2 tablespoons olive oil
- Salt and pepper to taste

Instructions:

In a large pot, heat olive oil and sauté onion, garlic, and ginger until softened. Add chicken cubes and cook until browned. Stir in garam masala, turmeric, and cumin, and cook for 1 minute. Add diced tomatoes and butter, stirring to melt the butter. Pour in heavy cream and bring to a simmer. Cook for 20 minutes or until the chicken is tender and the stew has thickened. Season with salt and pepper before serving.

French Provençal Stew (Daube)

Ingredients:

- 2 lbs beef stew meat, cubed
- 1 cup red wine
- 4 cups beef broth
- 2 medium onions, chopped
- 3 cloves garlic, minced
- 2 carrots, diced
- 2 medium tomatoes, chopped
- 1/4 cup olives, pitted
- 1 teaspoon dried thyme
- 1 tablespoon fresh rosemary, chopped
- 2 tablespoons olive oil
- Salt and pepper to taste

Instructions:

In a large pot, heat olive oil and brown the beef cubes on all sides. Remove and set aside. In the same pot, sauté onion, garlic, and carrots until softened. Stir in thyme, rosemary, tomatoes, olives, red wine, and beef broth. Return beef to the pot, bring to a boil, then reduce heat to a simmer. Cook for 2 hours, or until the beef is tender. Season with salt and pepper before serving.

Smoky Black Bean Stew

Ingredients:

- 2 cans black beans, drained and rinsed
- 1 medium onion, chopped
- 3 cloves garlic, minced
- 1 teaspoon smoked paprika
- 1 teaspoon cumin
- 1 teaspoon chili powder
- 4 cups vegetable broth
- 1 tablespoon olive oil
- Salt and pepper to taste

Instructions:

In a large pot, heat olive oil and sauté onion and garlic until softened. Stir in smoked paprika, cumin, and chili powder, and cook for another minute. Add black beans and vegetable broth, and bring to a boil. Reduce heat and simmer for 20–25 minutes, or until the stew thickens slightly. Season with salt and pepper before serving.

Crab and Corn Stew

Ingredients:

- 1 lb crab meat (fresh or canned)
- 2 cups corn kernels (fresh or frozen)
- 1 medium onion, chopped
- 3 cloves garlic, minced
- 4 cups seafood or chicken broth
- 1 cup heavy cream
- 2 tablespoons butter
- 1/2 teaspoon Old Bay seasoning
- Salt and pepper to taste

Instructions:

In a large pot, melt butter and sauté onion and garlic until softened. Add corn and Old Bay seasoning, and cook for 5 minutes. Stir in crab meat, seafood broth, and heavy cream. Bring to a boil, then reduce heat and simmer for 15–20 minutes, or until the flavors meld together. Season with salt and pepper before serving.

Hearty Meatball Stew

Ingredients:

- 1 lb ground beef or pork
- 1/2 cup breadcrumbs
- 1/4 cup grated Parmesan cheese
- 1 egg
- 2 teaspoons dried oregano
- 2 tablespoons parsley, chopped
- 4 cups beef broth
- 1 can diced tomatoes (14.5 oz)
- 2 medium carrots, diced
- 2 medium potatoes, peeled and cubed
- 1 onion, chopped
- 2 cloves garlic, minced
- 2 tablespoons olive oil
- Salt and pepper to taste

Instructions:

In a bowl, combine ground meat, breadcrumbs, Parmesan cheese, egg, oregano, parsley, salt, and pepper. Form into small meatballs. In a large pot, heat olive oil and brown the meatballs on all sides. Remove and set aside. In the same pot, sauté onion, garlic, carrots, and potatoes until softened. Add diced tomatoes, beef broth, and meatballs. Bring to a boil, then reduce heat and simmer for 30–40 minutes, or until the vegetables are tender and the meatballs are cooked through. Season with salt and pepper before serving.

Italian Polenta and Sausage Stew

Ingredients:

- 1 lb Italian sausage (bulk or casing removed)
- 1 cup polenta
- 4 cups chicken broth
- 1 can diced tomatoes (14.5 oz)
- 1 medium onion, chopped
- 2 cloves garlic, minced
- 1/2 cup Parmesan cheese, grated
- 2 tablespoons olive oil
- 1 teaspoon dried basil
- Salt and pepper to taste

Instructions:

In a large pot, heat olive oil and cook the sausage until browned, breaking it up into small pieces. Remove and set aside. In the same pot, sauté onion and garlic until softened. Stir in the diced tomatoes, chicken broth, and basil. Bring to a boil, then reduce heat to simmer. Slowly add the polenta, stirring constantly to avoid lumps. Continue to cook, stirring often, for about 20–25 minutes, until the polenta is tender. Stir in the sausage and Parmesan cheese. Season with salt and pepper before serving.

Spicy Tomato and Egg Stew

Ingredients:

- 4 large eggs
- 2 cups tomato sauce
- 1 can diced tomatoes (14.5 oz)
- 1 medium onion, chopped
- 3 cloves garlic, minced
- 1 teaspoon chili flakes (adjust to taste)
- 1 teaspoon paprika
- 1/2 teaspoon ground cumin
- 2 tablespoons olive oil
- Salt and pepper to taste

Instructions:

In a large pot, heat olive oil and sauté onion and garlic until softened. Stir in chili flakes, paprika, and cumin. Add diced tomatoes and tomato sauce, and bring to a simmer. Reduce the heat and let it cook for about 10–15 minutes, allowing the flavors to meld. Gently crack the eggs into the stew, cover, and cook for 5–7 minutes, or until the eggs are poached to your desired level of doneness. Season with salt and pepper before serving.

Jamaican Red Pea Stew

Ingredients:

- 1 lb dried red kidney beans (soaked overnight or quick-soaked)
- 1 medium onion, chopped
- 3 cloves garlic, minced
- 1 Scotch bonnet pepper, chopped (optional for heat)
- 1 tablespoon thyme
- 4 cups vegetable or chicken broth
- 1 can coconut milk (14 oz)
- 1 medium sweet potato, peeled and cubed
- 2 tablespoons vegetable oil
- Salt and pepper to taste

Instructions:

In a large pot, heat vegetable oil and sauté onion, garlic, and Scotch bonnet pepper (if using) until softened. Add the soaked red kidney beans, sweet potato, vegetable broth, thyme, and bring to a boil. Reduce the heat and simmer for about 1 hour, or until the beans are tender. Add coconut milk and continue to simmer for an additional 10 minutes. Season with salt and pepper before serving.

Persian Lamb and Apricot Stew

Ingredients:

- 1 lb lamb shoulder, cubed
- 1 onion, chopped
- 2 cloves garlic, minced
- 1 cup dried apricots, chopped
- 2 tablespoons ground cinnamon
- 1 teaspoon ground cumin
- 1/2 teaspoon ground turmeric
- 4 cups lamb broth or chicken broth
- 2 tablespoons olive oil
- Salt and pepper to taste

Instructions:

In a large pot, heat olive oil and brown the lamb cubes on all sides. Remove and set aside. In the same pot, sauté onion and garlic until softened. Stir in cinnamon, cumin, and turmeric, and cook for 1 minute. Add the lamb back into the pot along with apricots and broth. Bring to a boil, then reduce heat and simmer for 1–1.5 hours, or until the lamb is tender. Season with salt and pepper before serving.

Roasted Cauliflower and Coconut Stew

Ingredients:

- 1 head cauliflower, chopped into florets
- 1 can coconut milk (14 oz)
- 4 cups vegetable broth
- 1 medium onion, chopped
- 2 cloves garlic, minced
- 1 teaspoon ground cumin
- 1/2 teaspoon turmeric
- 2 tablespoons olive oil
- Salt and pepper to taste

Instructions:

Preheat the oven to 400°F (200°C). Toss cauliflower florets in olive oil, cumin, turmeric, salt, and pepper, and spread them on a baking sheet. Roast for 25–30 minutes, or until tender and slightly browned. In a large pot, sauté onion and garlic until softened. Add roasted cauliflower, coconut milk, and vegetable broth, and bring to a boil. Reduce the heat and simmer for 15–20 minutes. Use an immersion blender to blend the soup until smooth (or blend in batches). Season with salt and pepper before serving.

Wild Mushroom and Herb Stew

Ingredients:

- 1 lb wild mushrooms (such as cremini, shiitake, or oyster), chopped
- 1 medium onion, chopped
- 2 cloves garlic, minced
- 1 tablespoon fresh thyme, chopped
- 4 cups vegetable broth
- 1/2 cup dry white wine
- 2 tablespoons olive oil
- 1/4 cup heavy cream (optional for richness)
- Salt and pepper to taste

Instructions:

In a large pot, heat olive oil and sauté onion and garlic until softened. Add the mushrooms and cook until they release their moisture and start to brown. Stir in thyme, vegetable broth, and white wine. Bring to a boil, then reduce the heat and simmer for 30–40 minutes, allowing the flavors to meld. For a creamier stew, stir in heavy cream. Season with salt and pepper before serving.